Garden Tools

by Alison Auch

Content and Reading Adviser: Mary Beth Fletcher, Ed.D.
Educational Consultant/Reading Specialist
The Carroll School, Lincoln, Massachusetts

COMPASS POINT BOOKS
Minneapolis, Minnesota

Compass Point Books
3109 West 50th Street, #115
Minneapolis, MN 55410

Visit Compass Point Books on the Internet at *www.compasspointbooks.com*
or e-mail your request to *custserv@compasspointbooks.com*

Photographs ©: Peter Beck/Corbis, cover; PhotoDisc, cover (top and right), 5, 7, 17; Bob Pool/Tom Stack & Associates, 4; Stockbyte, 6, 8, 12, 16; Comstock, 9; Rebecca McEwen/Petting Zoo Publications, 10; Phil Bulgasch, 11; Photo Network/Tom McCarthy, 13; Unicorn Stock Photos/Jim Shippee, 14; William H. Allen, Jr./Visuals Unlimited, 15; Unicorn Stock Photos/Ted Rose, 17; Skjold Photographs, 18; D. Yeske/ Visuals Unlimited, 20 (top); Jim Baron/The Image Finders, 20 (bottom); Ariel Skelley/Corbis, 21 (top); Macduff Everton/Corbis, 21 (bottom).

Project Manager: Rebecca Weber McEwen
Editors: Heidi Schoof and Patricia Stockland
Photo Researcher: Svetlana Zhurkina
Designer: Jaime Martens

Library of Congress Cataloging-in-Publication Data
Auch, Alison.
Garden tools / by Alison Auch.
p. cm. — (Spyglass books)
Includes bibliographical references (p.).
Contents: How does your garden grow?—Spade—Trowel—Bulb planter—Watering can—Sprinkler—Pruning shears—Rake—More garden helpers.
ISBN 0-7565-0448-1 (hardcover)
1. Garden tools—Juvenile literature. [1. Garden tools.
2. Gardening.] I. Title. II. Series.
SB454.8 .A83 2003
681'.7631—dc21 2002012625

Contents

NOTE: Glossary words are in ***bold*** the first time they appear.

How Does Your Garden Grow?

A garden is a ***special*** place where plants grow.
Garden tools can help you grow a garden of your own.

Gardening Hint

Most gardens are planted in the spring. They can grow into the fall.

Spade

A spade is a kind of shovel.

You can use a spade to dig in the dirt.

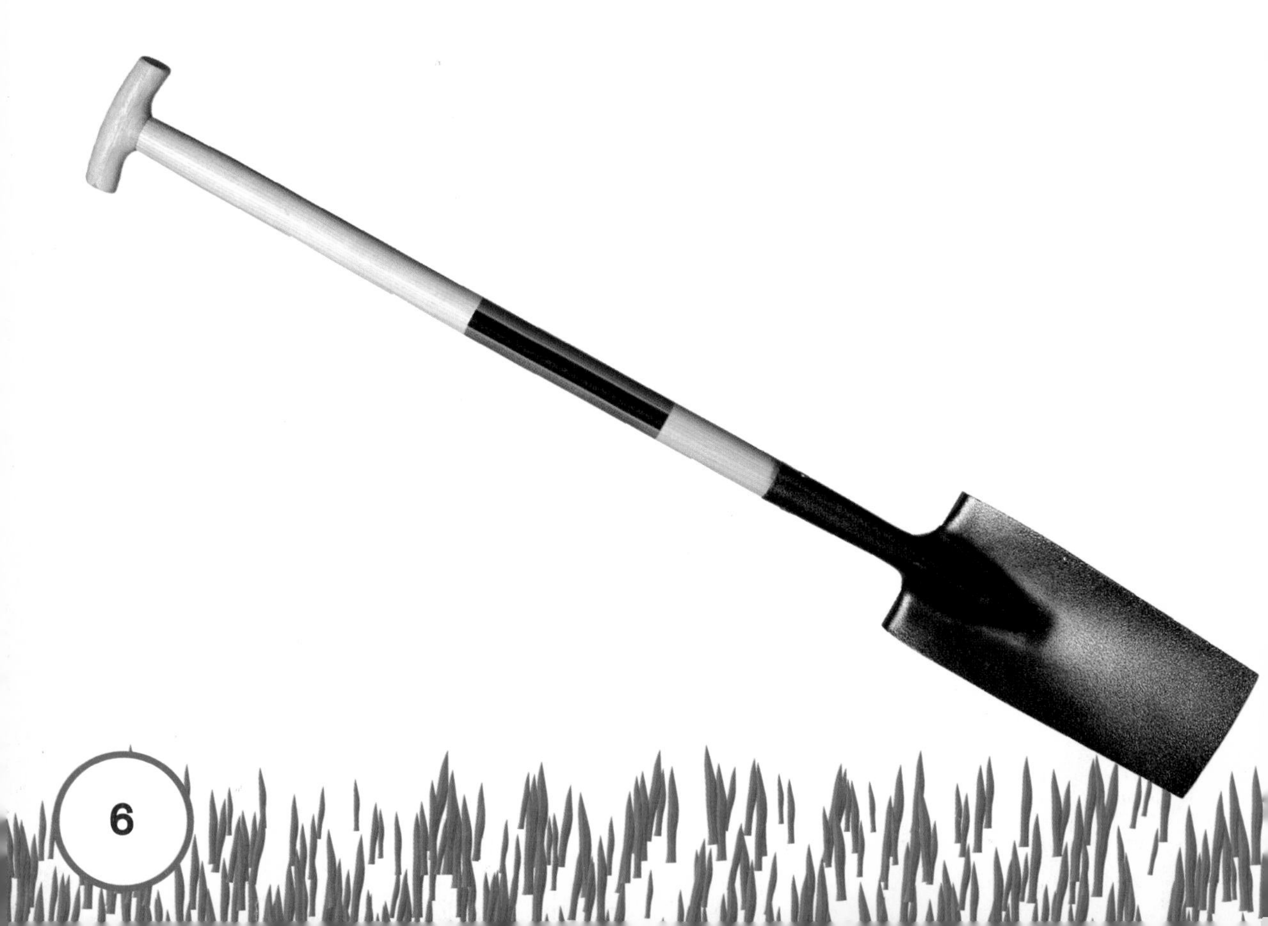

Gardening Hint

It is easiest to dig up garden dirt when it is a little bit wet.

Trowel

A trowel is a small shovel that you hold in your hand.

You can use a trowel to dig holes for your plants.

Gardening Hint

Trowels dig small holes. If you plant seeds, you can make smaller holes with your finger.

Bulb Planter

A ***bulb*** planter makes special holes for bulbs.

You can use a bulb planter to plant bulbs in your garden.

Gardening Hint

Most flower bulbs are planted in the fall. Then they bloom in the spring.

Watering Can

A watering can helps you ***sprinkle*** water over plants.

You can use a watering can after you plant your garden.

Gardening Hint

Plants and seeds need plenty of water to grow.

Sprinkler

A sprinkler ***sprays*** water from a hose.

You can use a sprinkler if you need to water a big garden.

Gardening Hint

It is best to water plants early in the morning or in the evening. This way, the sun won't dry up the water.

Pruning Shears

Pruning shears are like scissors with ***blades*** that can cut thick stems.

You can use pruning shears to ***trim*** your plants.

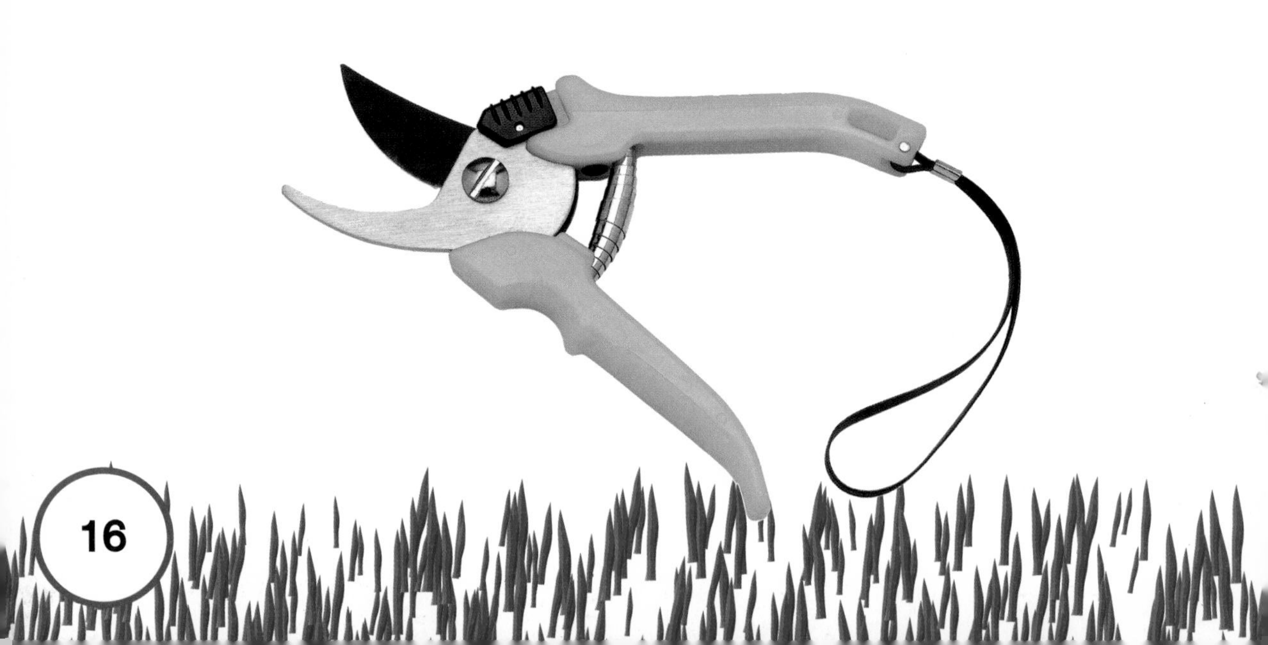

Gardening Hint

Make sure you ask an adult for help when your plants need to be pruned.

Rake

A rake has teeth that pull dead plants and leaves out of the garden.

You can use a rake to clean up your garden.

Gardening Hint

You can use a rake to cover seeds with a thin layer of dirt.

More Garden Helpers

Gardening gloves ***protect*** your hands from dirt and scrapes as you garden.

Seed packs show what the plants will look like and tell how to plant the seeds.

A hat can
protect you
from the sun
and help keep
you cool.

Plant markers can
show where you
planted things.
It's easy to forget!

Glossary

blade—the sharp, cutting part of a piece of metal

bulb—an onion-shaped part of a plant that grows underground and from which some plants grow

protect—to guard or keep something safe

special—not like the others

spray—to scatter liquid in very small drops

sprinkle—to scatter something in small drops or bits

trim—to cut small pieces off something

Learn More

Books

Eclare, Melanie. *A Harvest of Color: Growing a Vegetable Garden.* Brooklyn, N.Y.: Ragged Bear, 2002.

Maass, Robert. *Garden.* New York: Henry Holt, 1998.

MacLeod, Elizabeth. *Grow It Again.* Illustrated by Caroline Price. Toronto: Kids Can Press, 1999.

Web Sites

Kid's Valley Garden

www.raw-connections.com/garden/

My First Garden

www.urbanext.uiuc.edu/firstgarden/fundamentals/index.html

Index

GR: G
Word Count: 165

From Alison Auch

Reading and writing are my favorite things to do. When I'm not reading or writing, I like to go to the mountains or play with my little girl, Chloe.